SHIRE NATURAL H

of the ̀ ı ısles

A. A. WARDHAUGH

CONTENTS

Introduction 2
Flight and echolocation 3
Feeding and diet 7
Life cycle 10
The British bat species 14
Bat study and conservation 21
Further reading 24

Cover: *Leisler's Bat (Nyctalus leisleri).*

Series editor: Jim Flegg.

Copyright © 1987 and1995 by A. A. Wardhaugh.
First published 1987; reprinted 1990; second edition 1995.
Number 15 in the Shire Natural History series. ISBN 0 7478 0303 X.

British Library Cataloguing in Publication Data
Wardhaugh, A. A. Bats of the British Isles.
1.— Great Britain 2. Mammals — Great Britain. I. Title 599. 4'0941 QL737.C5

Printed in Great Britain by CIT Printing Services,
Press Buildings, Merlins Bridge, Haverfordwest, Dyfed SA61 1XF.

Introduction

Bats have a combination of two skills which makes them unique: they can fly and they can do so in complete darkness by using echolocation. These characteristics affect almost every aspect of their bodily design and are the key to their success. Bats are the only vertebrates that fly at night and feed on nocturnal insects caught on the wing. As a result of this unique lifestyle they have become a most diverse and successful group of animals. Bats are distributed throughout every region of the world except the poles and range in size from the world's smallest known mammal, the Hog-nosed Bat *(Craseonycteris thonglongyai)* of Thailand, with a mass of 2.0 grams (0.071 ounces) or less, to the fruit bats of the genus *Pteropus*, which can attain a wingspan of 2 metres (6 feet 7 inches) and a mass of 1 kilogram (2.2 pounds).

Bats have been evolving and diversifying for more than fifty million years. With the advent of man bats came to be regarded in the west as supernatural and to be associated with witchcraft because of their lifestyle. Consequently, although quite harmless, bats have suffered unnecessary persecution in the past and are still feared by many people and poorly understood. Since 1981 all British bats have benefited from legal protection. This has helped to increase public awareness of their decline in numbers due to human activities and to generate sympathy for these inoffensive and little-known creatures.

CLASSIFICATION

Bats possess fur and suckle their young. For these reasons and others they are classified as mammals. The class Mammalia contains about 4,100 species and is divided into a series of eighteen major groups called orders. The bats, or Chiroptera (meaning 'hand wing'), form one such order and with 950 species they are outnumbered in types only by the rodents. Bats fall into two main groups. The fruit bats (suborder Megachiroptera; about 175 species) are tropical and subtropical in distribution.

They are often large with proportionately big eyes and most but not all species eat fruits. Members of the other group (suborder Microchiroptera; about 775 species) are generally smaller, as their scientific name implies. They are mostly insectivorous, using echolocation for navigation and for finding their food by night. Their muzzles are short and their eyes are proportionately small. Unlike the Megachiroptera they never possess a claw on the second finger and species of more temperate latitudes spend the winter in hibernation.

The Microchiroptera are divided into seventeen families but only two of these have representatives in the British Isles, the consequence of a cool temperate climate and isolation from continental Europe. The two families are the Rhinolophidae (meaning 'nose protuberance'), which includes the Greater and Lesser Horseshoe Bats *(Rhinolophus ferrumequinum and R. hipposideros)*, and the Vespertilionidae ('of the evening'), which contains Britain's twelve remaining resident species. All fourteen species occur in the south of England but, because of the colder climate and perhaps lack of suitable habitats, only two or three are found in northern Scotland and seven in Ireland.

Bats probably appeared on earth not long, in geological terms, after the extinction of the dinosaurs. The oldest known fossil bat, Icaronycteris, is from early Eocene strata in Wyoming, USA, dated at fifty million years before the present. This and some other fossils almost as old are extremely well preserved and show that the animals were very similar to present-day species. Thus there have been bats on earth for more than ten times as long as there have been human beings. In common with other terrestrial organisms not normally inhabiting coastal or estuarine environments, fossilised bats are few and no intermediate stages in their evolution have yet been found. It is thought that bats evolved from primitive insectivores, the ancestors of today's shrews, moles and hedgehogs. Except for their flight adaptations bats are structurally quite similar to insectivores, notably in their dentition and digestive system. Presumably some of these primitive insectivores began living in trees, like today's tree shrews, and then learnt to catch flying insects by jumping from branch to branch. Extension of the body wall to form a gliding membrane as found in present-day flying squirrels would have been of great value. The inclusion of the hand and lengthening of the finger bones to support the wing would also have allowed alteration in its shape and, ultimately active, flapping flight. Presumably during this process the echolocating mechanism developed or became much refined. Some present-day insectivores have the capacity to echolocate.

It had been thought that the fruit bats were a subsequent offshoot from this evolutionary line but investigations published in 1986 indicated that the organisation of their optic tracts and of the visual centre of the brain is highly complex and, moreover, strikingly similar to the arrangement in primates. This pointed to the uncomfortable conclusion that fruit bats might have evolved independently, from primitive primate stock and that they are unrelated to the Microchiroptera. However, more recent studies on similarities and differences in the DNA of the three groups supports the view that bats do form a unified order, originating from an insectivorous ancestor.

Flight and echolocation

STRUCTURE AND FLIGHT

The chief structural specialisation possessed by bats is the wings but many other aspects of their bodily design are adaptations for flight. The wing is supported by greatly elongated arm, hand and finger bones, the membrane being a fold of skin just 0.03 mm thick (about 1.2 thousandths of an inch) in small species, yet surprisingly strong. During embryonic development it grows outward from the flank and when fully formed it begins at the shoulder, runs to the base of the thumb and includes the fingers, the hind legs and in most species the tail. Being a double layer of skin containing blood vessels and nerves, the wing membrane is a living structure and small tears will heal quickly. It also contains elastic fibres and small muscles which help to keep the extended wing taut during flight and aid folding when it is closed. Within the wing the humerus and radius are large and strong but the ulna is reduced and fused with the radius. The wrist bones are

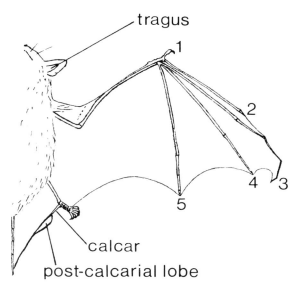

1. Bat structure. A Pipistrelle *(Pipistrellus pipistrellus)*. 1, thumb; 2-5, second to fifth fingers.

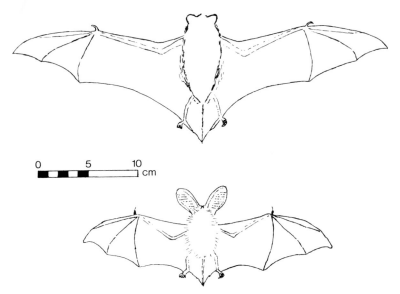

2. *Wing shape of the Noctule (Nyctalus noctula) and Brown Long-eared Bat (Plecotus auritus) compared.*

much fused, allowing spreading of the fingers to alter wing shape but no twisting of the hand. The thumb is short and strong and bears a claw used for gripping when the bat crawls.

As in birds, wing shape varies. Slow-flying species such as the Brown Long-eared Bat *(Plecotus auritus)* have short, broad wings whilst fast fliers such as the Noctule *(Nyctalus noctula)* possess longer, narrower wings. When flying, the wing is partly folded during the upstroke, lifted above the back and then extended fully for the downstroke. The number of beats per second varies between species but is generally about ten to twenty. Unlike birds, bats do not seem to soar or glide for extended periods of time. Because of the way in which wing shape can be varied, bats are highly manoeuvrable in flight and since no air can pass through the membrane they do not have the problem of drifting encountered by birds. The tail membrane can be curved forwards and acts chiefly as an air brake, for example when landing. It does not seem to have a significant function in steering. The edge of the tail membrane is supported by a spur of cartilage called the *calcar* which is attached to the heel. On its outer edge there is in some species a membrane called the *post-calcarial lobe*. This can be a valuable identification feature in the field, as can the shape of the *tragus* or inner ear.

Apart from the wings, bats have numerous other adaptations for flight. The neck is short, which helps to keep the body mass around the centre of gravity. The large thorax and tapering abdomen provide a streamlined shape. As in birds, the breast bone has a keel for the attachment of flight muscles. The stout collar bones are rigidly attached to this and to the shoulder blades, transmitting thrust from the wings to the rest of the body via the rigid, box-like rib cage. The pelvic girdle is open at the front so that the socket for the femur faces outwards and upwards. This arrangement is necessary because the legs are incorporated into the wing membrane and are therefore widely spaced. Even the fur shows some adaptation to flight. The slow-flying Brown Long-

4

3. Pipistrelle (Pipistrellus pipistrellus).

eared Bat has longish fur but that of the Noctule is short, sleek and glossy, undoubtedly reducing resistance to the air. Flight is very strenuous and the proportionately large heart can beat a thousand times a minute in small species, with blood completing a circuit through the lungs and body in about two seconds. The blood of bats is able to absorb 27 per cent by volume of oxygen compared with 18 per cent in other mammals.

The feet have five toes, each bearing a claw. A tendon running from the third toe bone to the claw base is so arranged that under the weight of the body it pulls the claw forward. In this way resting bats can suspend themselves by their feet without any muscular effort.

4. Brown Long-eared Bat (Plecotus auritus).

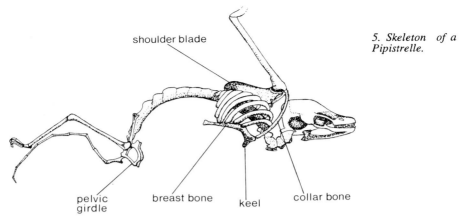

shoulder blade

5. *Skeleton of a Pipistrelle.*

pelvic girdle

breast bone

keel

collar bone

ECHOLOCATION

At night, light from car headlamps is reflected back from the road and other nearby objects, thereby reaching the eyes of the driver, where an image is formed. Echolocation operates in the same way but the medium involved is sound not light. Bats produce a series of very rapid sound pulses and, by listening for any returning echoes, they are able to build up a mental picture of their surroundings. Sound reflected from a nearby object will return sooner and be louder than that returning from a more distant one. A hard, continuous surface such as a cave wall will produce a sharper echo than a softer surface such as foliage. Small objects to one side of the head can be pinpointed because returning sound waves will reach the two ears at fractionally different times and be of different intensities. In this way bats can form a detailed sound image of their surroundings. In particular, they can locate, track and capture night-flying insects.

Although bats can produce squeaks, chirps and other sounds audible to the human ear, those used for echolocation are of a very high frequency (generally 35,000 to 60,000 hertz), well above the range of human hearing (20 to 20,000 hertz). The voice box is large and strengthened with bone so that great tension can be maintained on the vocal cords in order to produce the high-frequency vibrations required. In addition, the inner ear is large and highly developed. High-frequency sounds are the most appropriate for echolocation because their wavelengths are very short, as little as

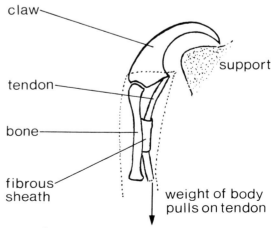

claw

tendon

bone

fibrous sheath

support

weight of body pulls on tendon

6. *Claw mechanism.*

6

Feeding and diet

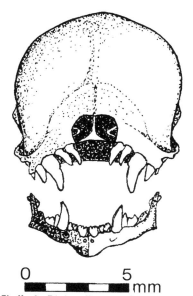

7. *Skull of a Pipistrelle viewed from the front. Note the large gap between the upper incisors, thought to be important for the emission of ultrasound pulses.*

All the British bat species normally spend the daytime at their roost sites resting and then emerge to feed at dusk. Roost sites fall into three main categories: holes in trees; caves, disused mines and similar places; and buildings. Both the nature of the site and the number of individuals present varies with species and the time of year. The following is a general account of feeding and further details are given in the species descriptions.

During the summer months bats emerge to feed shortly after sunset, a time when many insects are active. After one or two hours they rest, either at the daytime roost site or elsewhere. Often they will feed again for a period just before dawn. Not all individuals feed every night. If the weather is cold, wet or windy bats seem reluctant to emerge, probably because so few insects would be caught that the energy gained would be less than that expended on flight. The number of individuals at a roost site varies but fifty to a hundred is not unusual for a summer Pipistrelle *(Pipistrellus pipistrellus)* roost in the eaves of a modern house. On leaving at dusk the bats move off purposefully to preferred feeding areas often some distance from the roost site. They spread out and each bat seems to have a definite feeding territory, for example part of a woodland edge or a row of gardens. Here they will often repeatedly fly the same path, catching insects on the wing.

Most species seem to eat their prey in flight but some, such as the Brown Long-eared Bat and the horseshoe bats, carry food to a perch often at or near the roost site before devouring it. Discarded moth wings and other insect remains can sometimes be found below such sites. In flight bats are able to make use of the wings and tail membrane in prey capture. The wings can be flexed and the tail membrane curled forward in order to scoop up flying insects, which are then transferred to the mouth. This seems to be a deliberate action: the

1.6 mm (0.06 inch), and therefore suitable for producing echoes from small objects, such as insects. The sounds are produced in a concentrated beam through the mouth by most species and there is a large gap between the upper incisors to facilitate this. The horseshoe bats, however, emit ultrasound through their noses and the peculiarly shaped nose leaf is thought to help concentrate the stream of sound pulses. Using echolocation vespertilionid bats can perceive insects up to one metre (about one yard) away but horseshoe bats can detect objects at ten times this distance. The ability to echo-locate is very much a characteristic of the Microchiroptera. With only a very few exceptions, the fruit bats do not have this capability.

Little is known about the other senses of bats. It is thought that the Microchiroptera can see only nearby objects and are better able to perceive moving rather than static ones. Their tactile sense may be good, judging by the presence of whiskers and also sensory hairs on the ears and wings.

8. Noctule (Nyctalus noctula).

9. Daubenton's Bat (Myotis daubentoni).

10. Whiskered Bat (Myotis mystacinus) at hibernation site.

11. Brandt's Bat (Myotis brandtii).

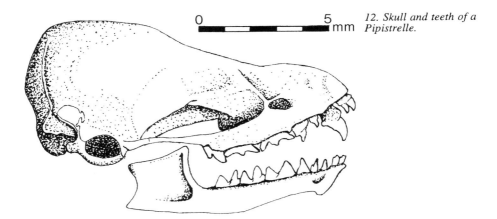

0 ▬▬▬▬▬▬ 5 mm   *12. Skull and teeth of a Pipistrelle.*

wings are not simply used as dragnets. Being small creatures, bats have a proportionately large surface area for their volume and so lose body heat very rapidly. It is essential for them to eat enough food to counteract this loss and small bats consume up to 25 per cent of their body mass in insects during one feeding session. For a Pipistrelle this would be about three thousand midges or their equivalent. Hence during the course of one summer a colony of a hundred bats will devour tens of millions of insects.

The teeth are typically those of an insectivorous animal. The sharp incisors and canines are able to bite and grip and the cusped cheek teeth cut and break up the food. Very little is known about precisely which insect species are eaten. In general the range in size of insects taken seems to vary with the size of the bat. Only larger species such as the Noctule eat crickets and large beetles, for example. Analysis of insect remains within bat droppings is possible, although not easy, and probably much could be learnt from this approach. Diet may well vary through the year as it does for martins and swallows.

All British bats are insectivorous, as are 70 per cent of the world's bat species. Fruit bats are restricted to tropical regions because only a hot, non-seasonal climate will provide them with food throughout the year. They chew and crush their food, consuming the nutritious fluid and rejecting tough, fibrous material. A few bats feed on nectar and pollen and are similarly restricted to the tropics. Others eat fish, amphibians, lizards and small rodents. Finally there are the vampire bats, three small New World species which use their razor-sharp teeth to bite the necks, ears and legs of birds and mammals such as horses and cattle. Their saliva contains an anticoagulant so that the small wound will bleed for some time, giving the bats ample opportunity to lap up the blood. Unfortunately these bats can transmit rabies, which is much more harmful than the bite inflicted.

Life cycle

Like the daily feeding routine, the annual life cycle follows a general pattern in British species. From October to March bats hibernate, often in caves or similar places. They awake in the spring and move to warmer summer sites. Males remain solitary or in small groups but females often gather together to form quite large colonies of a hundred or more individuals. Here the young are born and grow rapidly. Mating usually takes place in the autumn.

One unique part of this cycle is that, following mating, sperm are stored within the body of the female for several months, including the hibernation period. The female does not produce ova until the following spring and only then does fertilisation occur. The reason for this unusual arrangement is that males probably require a period of warmth in order to reach breeding condition and hence may not be able to effect a fertile mating soon after hibernation.

Whether a female becomes pregnant depends at least partly on the spring weather and consequent food supply, but little is known of the exact mechanisms involved. Cold periods will cause the animal to become torpid, slowing down development of the embryo, hence the duration of pregnancy is variable. Females seek out very warm summer roosts, such as south-facing house eaves in the case of the Pipistrelle, and the single young is born in late June or July. During birth the female often turns head upwards so that the baby is delivered into the cradling tail membrane. At birth the offspring may already be 25 per cent of the adult mass. Twins have rarely been recorded in Britain but are more frequent in some species (for example, the Pipistrelle and Noctule) in other parts of Europe, perhaps in response to a consistently warm spring and hence a more reliable food supply.

Babies are looked after with great care and suckled regularly. If lost at the roost site, young bats can emit a high-pitched isolation call, to which the mother responds by intensive searching until the baby is found. Ultrasound production develops from this isolation call at a later age. Normally the offspring are left behind each night when the females emerge to feed but they can be carried, clinging to the underside of the mother's body, if the group changes its roost site. The young develop very rapidly and, although blind and virtually hairless at birth, they are almost fully grown at three weeks old. At about this time they take their first flight, a skill which seems to be largely innate but no doubt improves much through practice.

The young become independent by late summer and, like the adults, must feed well during autumn in order to build up energy reserves for hibernation. At this time bats can steadily increase their body mass by up to 35 per cent. Mostly British species do not become mature until the autumn of their second year. Bats are surprisingly long-lived, with ages of up to eleven years recorded for the Pipistrelle and over thirty years for a number of other British species.

HIBERNATION

During poor weather bats can become torpid, that is they allow their body temperature to fall with that of their surroundings. This is a valuable adaptation since their bodily functions slow down, so reducing the consumption of vital energy reserves. Bats can economise on energy use by becoming torpid during the daytime even when the weather is quite warm. Hibernation is an extension of this process, the sites chosen for it being humid and cool but frost-free. Depending upon species, caves, disused mines, cellars, ice-houses and tree cavities are sites often used. Should conditions in the hibernaculum become unsuitable, for example too hot or too cold, bodily mechanisms cause the bats to waken so that they can move to a different locality.

Waking takes some time, body temperature rising by only one degree Celsius every two minutes. Thus it can take up to an hour for a hibernating bat to become fully active. Such waking uses up a considerable amount of energy and hibernating bats should never be disturbed. The energy loss incurred could leave them with insufficient reserves with which to survive the winter. The northerly distribution of some species in Europe may be limited by the extent to which they are able to let their body temperature fall during hibernation.

Some North American bat species undertake migratory movements in order to avoid the extremes of winter weather. In Europe regular movements of bats up to 100 km (62 miles) southward for hibernation are known but detailed information on British bats is lacking. Occasionally animals have been found on ships and offshore installations, suggesting migratory movements, but these individuals could represent emigration movements resulting from population pressures.

13. Natterer's Bat (Myotis nattereri).

14. Serotine (Eptesicus serotinus).

15. *Lesser and Greater Horseshoe Bats (Rhinolophus hipposideros and R. ferrumequinum). The Greater Horsehoe (right) measures about 90 mm (3¹/₂ inches) from head to toe.*

16. *Greater Horsehoe Bat (Rhinolophus ferrumequinum).*

The British bat species

Species are not dealt with in a systematic manner but the commonest and most widespread types are described first, progressing to the more restricted and rarer species at the end.

PIPISTRELLE, *Pipistrellus pipistrellus* (figs. 1, 3, 5, 7).

The Pipistrelle ranges throughout Britain and is the most likely species to be encountered by the casual observer. It can often be seen feeding in suburban areas and city parks shortly after sunset, when it flies just above head height twisting and turning rapidly as it catches insects.

The Pipistrelle is the smallest British bat, the head and body being about 38 mm (1¹/₂ inches) long and the wingspan 200 to 230 mm (8 to 9 inches). Mass varies during the year but is not more than 7.5 grams (¹/₄ ounce). The fur is red-brown to dark brown, usually slightly paler below. The ears are short, bluntly rounded and almost triangular in shape, the tragus being longer than broad and also bluntly rounded. A postcalcarial lobe is present.

Recently, it has been found that the Pipistrelle occurs in two distinct forms which may well be different species. One, the 'bandit pipistrelle', has a black face and dark brown fur whilst the 'brown pipistrelle' has a brown face and fur of a more chestnut brown. The two forms also differ in the frequency at which they echolocate.

Pipistrelles are active from March to October or November, probably the longest period for any British bat, and a study in East Anglia showed that they habitually feed on winter nights if the temperature is above 8 C (48 F). In summer female nursing colonies frequently roost in modern houses, for example behind soffits and barge-boards or hanging tiles, but not normally in loft spaces. Being so small, Pipistrelles can easily enter through a gap of just 12 mm (¹/₂ inch). Such sites are occupied between May and August but Pipistrelles are prone to change site and often do not stay in one place for the whole of this period. Pipistrelles are known to travel 5 km (3 miles) to preferred feeding sites so their presence does not necessarily indicate a roost nearby.

BROWN LONG-EARED BAT, *Plecotus auritus* (figs. 2, 4).

If seen clearly, this bat is easily recognisable by its huge ears, which are nearly as long as the head and body combined. Woodland, established parkland and similar areas are the preferred habitats. It can be seen from around thirty minutes after sunset, often flying slowly around tree canopies, where it has the characteristic habit of feeding by taking insects from the leaves, sometimes hovering as it does so.

The ears are so large because the ultrasound pulses produced for echolocation are very quiet. They are therefore sensitive enough to distinguish between an insect and the leaf on which it rests, something other bats probably cannot do. In flight this quiet echolocation may also allow the long-eared bat to catch certain moth species which are capable of detecting the louder ultrasound of other bats. In response these insects evade capture by a zigzag flight or by closing their wings and dropping quickly out of the bat's flight path. Some moths, for example the tiger moths (Arctiidae), have developed the ability to emit ultrasound themselves in order to disorientate would-be predators. Moths do, however, form a significant part of the diet, notably noctuids such as the Large Yellow Underwing *(Noctua pronuba)*, and discarded wings can sometimes be found beneath a favourite feeding perch. Brown Long-eared Bats generally seem to stay within about one kilometre (1100 yards) of their roost site when feeding.

Apart from its ears, this delicately built species is only a little larger than the Pipistrelle. The long, thick fur is brown, being paler below. The head and body are up to about 50 mm (2 inches) long and the long, broad wings have a span of up to 270 mm (11 inches). For a bat, the eyes are relatively large. The ears are rounded at the tip, with conspicuous transverse folds, and joined at the bases.

At rest they are curled backwards and

17. Grey Long-eared Bat
(*Plecotus austriacus*).

tucked beneath the wings, probably to help prevent heat loss through their large surface. At such times the tragus, which is about half the length of the ear, remains projecting and could easily be mistaken for the ear itself.

In summer females form nursery roosts, usually of up to forty individuals, and they often inhabit the lofts or attics of older houses, where by contrast to most other British bats they often occupy exposed positions, such as along the ridge beam. This species is quite common and widely distributed. It is probably rarer in the Scottish Highlands but occurs in Ireland. The only species with which it might be confused is the far rarer Grey Long-eared bat.

GREY LONG-EARED BAT, *Plecotus austriacus* (fig. 17).

In Britain this species is known only from Dorset and Sussex. It is very slightly larger than its close relative the Brown Long-eared Bat and has a dark brown face in contrast to the pinkish brown face of the latter. As the name suggests, its fur is of a greyer hue but so too is the fur of young Brown Long-eared Bats. Little else is known about how the two species differ.

NOCTULE, *Nyctalus noctula* (figs. 2, 8, 24).

The Noctule is one of the largest British bats, with a wingspan of 350 mm (14 inches) or more. It occurs throughout England and Wales but is probably more thinly and locally distributed in the north, being absent from Scotland and Ireland. The Noctule is powerfully built with proportionately long, slender wings. Its flight is fast and dashing, reaching estimated speeds of up to 50 km/h (30 mph), triple that of the Pipistrelle. It emerges from its roost comparatively early and characteristically flies and feeds at considerable heights, sometimes uttering a high-pitched, clear call. The diet is thought to consist chiefly of beetles (notably Cockchafers), moths and smaller insects.

The bright chestnut fur of the adult is distinctive but juveniles are darker. The ears are widely spaced, the tragus being small, rounded and much narrower at the base than the tip. The Noctule does not normally inhabit buildings and the roost site is nearly always a tree cavity; it favours beech, oak and ash and sometimes takes over vacated woodpecker holes. Except when hibernating, Noctules change their roost site frequently and colonies have sev-

18. Bechstein's Bat (Myotis bechsteinii).

eral roosting sites within their range. In Britain this species continues to occupy tree cavities throughout the winter, hibernating from about October to late March. Other species with which the Noctule may be confused are Leisler's Bat and the Serotine.

DAUBENTON'S BAT, *Myotis daubentoni* (figs. 9, 21).

This species can be recognised by its habit of sometimes flying very low over still or slowly flowing water when feeding, occasionally taking an insect from the surface. It will plane just above the water, following a smoothly winding path for several metres with a distinctly shallow and quivering wing beat. Sometimes quite large numbers of individuals can be seen feeding in this way when there is a local abundance of food. The summer roost site can be in a crevice on the underside of a stone bridge or in similar positions in walls and buildings or else in a tree cavity, often near to water.

Daubenton's Bat is quite small, with a head and body about 50 mm (2 inches) long and a wingspan of about 250 mm (10 inches). The fur is warm to dark brown

above and grey buff below, the face being pinkish brown. The tragus is convexly curved on the posterior edge and is about half the length of the ear. There is no post-calcarial lobe and the feet are proportionately large, being about half as long as the shin. This species is probably quite widespread throughout Britain and occurs in Ireland.

WHISKERED BAT, *Myotis mystacinus* (figs. 10, 22).

It is not possible to distinguish this small species from the Pipistrelle when in flight with any degree of certainty. The longer, soft fur gives it a chubbier appearance in flight and it seems to fly more slowly and steadily. Unlike the Pipistrelle it does not utter any noise audible to the human ear when in flight.

The head and body are up to 50 mm (2 inches) long and the maximum wingspan is 240 mm (9½ inches). The fur varies from dark grey to grey-brown above and is off-white below, the muzzle being dark brown. As its name suggests, the lips bear long sensory hairs. No post-calcarial lobe is present on the wing. Compared with

19. Barbastelle (Barbastella barbastellus).

20. Mouse-eared Bat (Myotis myotis).

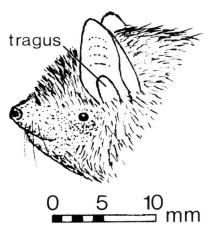

tragus

0 5 10 mm

21. Daubenton's Bat, showing the shape of the tragus, which has a convex posterior margin.

Daubenton's Bat, the tragus is straight and tapering and the ears are longer, reaching beyond the nostrils if held forward. The foot is smaller, being only a third the length of the shin. The only other species with which it may be confused when seen at close quarters is Brandt's Bat.

The Whiskered Bat haunts woodland sites, especially those with rivers or ponds. Summer roost sites can include tree cavities or older buildings where, like many species, it is often hidden from view, for example between roof tiles and underboarding or above ridge beams. Knowledge of its distribution is uncertain owing to confusion with Brandt's Bat but it is probably fairly widespread in England and Wales, present in Ireland but rare in Scotland.

BRANDT'S BAT, *Myotis brandtii* (fig. 11).

Recognised as a distinct species in the early 1970s, this animal is very similar indeed to the Whiskered Bat. On average it is slightly larger, with a wingspan of up to 255 mm (10 inches). Adults usually have rich red-brown fur, buff below, with a dark red-brown muzzle. Juveniles have grey-brown fur and are therefore very like the Whiskered Bat. Only minor differences in dentition and shape of the male genital organs serve to distinguish the species with any certainty. Nothing seems to be known about differences in their habits and distribution.

NATTERER'S BAT, *Myotis nattereri* (figs. 13, 23).

This is a medium-sized bat with a wingspan of up to 300 mm (12 inches) but it is not particularly easy to distinguish in flight from smaller species such as the Whiskered Bat or Pipistrelle. However, its whitish underparts are visible from a distance, if, for example, a resting individual is observed with the aid of a torch. When seen at close quarters there is a clear demarcation between this white fur and the grey-brown of the back. Natterer's Bat has a pinkish face with ears which are pink at the base, shading to brown at the tips. At 14 to 17 mm (about ⅝ inch long) they are proportionately longer than those of its smaller relative the Whiskered Bat and extend well beyond the tip of the nose if held forwards. The narrow, pointed tragus is two-thirds the length of the ear. Its most distinctive feature is the row of stiff hairs present along the edge of the tail membrane. These are about one millimetre long and arise from tiny swellings. They are present even in quite young animals.

This species haunts woodland and pasture, roosting during summer months in

22. Whiskered Bat, showing the shape of the tragus, which is straight and tapering.

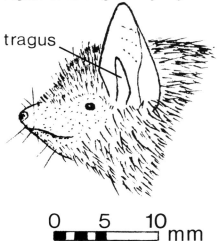

tragus

0 5 10 mm

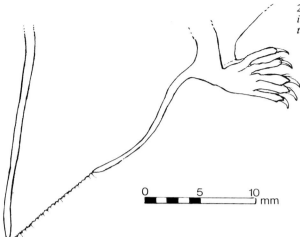

23. *Young Natterer's Bat, showing the row of stiff bristles along the margin of the tail membrane.*

tree cavities and old, relatively undisturbed buildings such as churches, tucked away in confined spaces. Its distribution is poorly known but it probably occurs throughout the British Isles including Ireland. It may be more thinly distributed in Northern England and Scotland.

SEROTINE, *Eptesicus serotinus* (fig. 14).

The Serotine is one of the larger British species. With a wingspan of about 380 mm (15 inches), it is similar in size to the Noctule but is much broader-winged and slower in flight. Like the Noctule it can ascend to considerable heights when feeding but often flies much closer to the ground. This species is restricted to the southern half of England and Wales and has not been recorded in Ireland.

The Serotine has dark red-brown fur with paler underparts. However, some individuals can be generally darker. The ears are small and rounded with a tragus which, in contrast to those of the Noctule and Leisler's Bat, is longer than broad. The teeth are relatively long and strong, suited to its diet of large moths and beetles. In summer this species seems very dependent on houses, usually older ones where it occupies sites similar to the Pipistrelle. Nursing colonies usually contain fifteen to thirty individuals. In Britain buildings are probably also used for hibernation since there are very few records of Serotines retiring to caves for the winter months.

LEISLER'S BAT, *Nyctalus leisleri* (cover).

This species is a smaller relative of the Noctule, with a wingspan of about 300 mm (12 inches). It is uncommon in England and has not been recorded from Scotland or Wales. It is quite common in Ireland, where the Noctule is absent.

Like the Noctule, Leisler's Bat is a fast, high-flying species favouring wooded districts, sometimes even large parks. It roosts in old decayed trees but is also known to inhabit buildings. There have been few studies of its behaviour but it has been reported to fiy more steadily when feeding, making only shallow dives to catch insects, in contrast to the steep plunges of the Noctule. It may be rather more strictly nocturnal in its habits. The fur of the upper parts is golden-brown, becoming a little paler and greyer below, in all slightly darker than that of the Noctule. In contrast to the latter, the bases of the hairs are dark, notably those of the underside.

LESSER HORSESHOE BAT, *Rhinolophus hipposideros* (fig. 15).

This now uncommon species is a little

19

24. Noctule bat being examined during the course of conservation work. This and similar-sized species must be handled carefully since they can deliver a painful bite. Smaller bats such as the Pipistrelle do not have jaws and teeth powerful enough to penetrate human skin.

more widespread than its larger relative the Greater Horseshoe Bat, occurring chiefly in south-west England, Wales and western Ireland. In the nineteenth century it occurred as far north as Ripon in North Yorkshire.

Both species of horseshoe bat are broad-winged, slow-flying and capable of hovering. They have weak legs and are not able to crawl but hang upside down by their toes, in exposed positions such as cave roofs, often with the wings wrapped around the body. This is in line with popular beliefs about bats but unusual among British species. The ears are broad and pointed, lacking a tragus. One of the most characteristic features is the nose leaf, used to concentrate sounds produced for echolocation.

The Lesser Horseshoe Bat has dark grey-brown fur, paler below, and a wingspan of up to 250 mm (10 inches). Both this species and its larger relative have been found to occupy caves and buildings during both summer and winter. They do not become sexually mature until four years old, unlike other British species, which can commence breeding at two years. Females bear two false teats on the abdomen, in addition to the functional pair, which offer further

opportunity for the offspring to secure itself if carried by the mother in flight. The young of other British bats develop hooked milk teeth with which they can grip the parent's fur but in horseshoe bats milk teeth never appear.

GREATER HORSESHOE BAT, *Rhinolophus ferrumequinum* (figs. 15, 16).

This species has declined greatly in numbers since the nineteenth century, when there were probably over ten thousand individuals in Britain. Now the population is no more than a few hundred, restricted to south-west England and south Wales. This is probably due to loss of roost sites and suitable feeding habitats, notably unimproved pasture.

The Greater Horseshoe Bat has a wingspan of up to 380 mm (15 inches), the fur being medium to light brown above, greyer and paler below. It characteristically flies and feeds quite low, often within 3 metres (10 feet) of the ground, occasionally gliding. Diet includes larger beetles, notably Cockchafers in spring and Dor Beetles later in the year. In winter it will sometimes emerge from hibernation to feed if the night temperature rises above 10 C (50 F).

BARBASTELLE, *Barbastella barbastellus* (fig. 19).

This is a rare species in Britain. It is commoner in the south than the north and probably absent from Scotland and Ireland. The Barbastelle is a medium-sized, slow-flying bat with a wingspan of about 280 mm (11 inches). At close quarters it is very distinctive since the large, broad ears meet over the forehead. Only the long-eared bats have the same characteristic but their enormous ears make them easy to distinguish. The fur is dark brown, nearly black, with a few hairs having pale tips, giving a frosted appearance. This is a woodland species, being solitary or found in small numbers. It roosts in trees or, occasionally, buildings.

BECHSTEIN'S BAT, *Myotis bechsteinii* (fig. 18).

This bat is one of Britain's rarest mammals with, on average, about one record of its occurrence each year. It is restricted to the southern half of England, chiefly Devon, Somerset, Dorset, Wiltshire and Hampshire. Bechstein's Bat is similar in appearance to its close relative, Natterer's Bat, although slightly larger. It lacks the row of stiff hairs along the tail membrane possessed by this species and has proportionately longer ears (18 to 26 mm, 3/4 to 1 inch long). These are surpassed in size only by those of the long-eared bats but in contrast their bases are not joined over the forehead. The fur is light brown above and pale grey below. Bechstein's Bat inhabits extensive areas of open woodland, roosting in tree cavities to a large extent. Such roosts are not easy to find so it may not be quite as rare as it seems.

MOUSE-EARED BAT, *Myotis myotis* (fig. 20).

This has always been a very uncommon species in Britain, evidence suggesting that it has not been a long term resident. Colonies were known in Dorset (1956-79) and Sussex (1969-90), both perhaps being founded by immigrants from continental Europe. If any unknown colonies are present they are likely to be in these or adjacent counties. The Mouse-eared Bat is declining generally in Europe. It is a large relative of the Whiskered and Natterer's Bats, with a wingspan of 365 to 450 mm (14¹/₂ to 18 inches). It has large, broad ears, the fur being grey-brown above and off-white below. Elsewhere in Europe it has been observed hunting for food on the ground, evidently seeking out dung beetles, other non-flying insects and spiders.

VAGRANTS

Six vagrant species have been recorded in Britain and others may occur. Nathusius' pipistrelle *(Pipistrellus nathusii)* has been identified on a number of occasions. It is very similar to the common Pipistrelle but slightly larger and noticeably paler below. Individuals of Kuhl's Pipistrelle *(P. kuhlii)* have been recorded in Jersey (1991) and Sussex (1992) and Savi's Pipistrelle *(P. savii)* in Sussex (1993). There have been a few records of the Parti-coloured Bat *(Vespertilio murinus)*, including two in different parts of Britain during the winter of 1985-6 and one in Essex in 1994. This is a medium to large species, white below and dark brown above, frosted with white. One specimen of the Hoary Bat *(Lasiurus cinereus)* was found in Scotland in 1847. This is a North American species comparable in size to the Noctule, having the tail membrane covered with fur. A male Northern Bat *(Eptesicus nilssonii)* was found at a hibernation site in Surrey in January 1987. Although not especially a migratory species, this may have been a displaced migrant from continental Europe.

Bat study and conservation

Contrary to the beliefs held by many people, British bat species are harmless creatures. They do not transmit disease to humans and when occupying buildings they do not construct any kind of nest, merely hanging from rafters or more often hiding in crevices, without causing any damage.

Their droppings, which consist chiefly of insect skeletons, dry rapidly, do not rot, do not corrode paintwork and are not a health hazard. Bats have no wish to become entangled in human hair and are far too skilful in flight to do so by accident. They deserve all the care and protection we can give them because some species, such as the Greater Horseshoe Bat, have suffered serious population declines and even the commoner species are probably not as numerous as in the past. The main causes have been loss of roost sites and suitable feeding habitats.

Before the advent of man, bats inhabited woodlands and river valleys, roosting in hollow trees and caves. As forests were cleared they took to living in buildings and also disused mines and similar places. During the twentieth century many roost sites have been lost, those in mines as a result of infilling or blockage of entrances for safety. Fortunately important roost sites in old mines are now sometimes conserved by the fitting of a grille over the entrance. Tree cavities are occupied by many creatures, including bats, but too often old decaying trees with suitable holes are felled during maintenance operations. Roost sites in buildings may be lost when access points are blocked, when wall cavities are filled for insulation or when retiling and underfelting is carried out. Probably the most serious threat comes from the remedial treatment of roof timbers, for example those infected with woodworm. Many of the chemicals used are highly persistent and lethal to bats, sometimes even if inhaled or contacted by the animals long after treatment has been carried out. Fortunately, much less toxic alternatives are now available for very little extra cost. Loss of feeding habitat has probably contributed significantly to the decline in bat populations. Destruction of permanent, unimproved pasture, hedgerows and woodlands and the canalisation of rivers have reduced the number and diversity of insects available as food in many areas. For example, the Greater Horseshoe Bat feeds chiefly on Cockchafers in spring and these insects are found mainly in areas of unimproved pasture.

Fortunately bats were afforded a good deal of protection by the 1981 Wildlife and Countryside Act. It is now illegal to kill, injure or even handle a wild bat of any species, to possess a bat or disturb a roosting bat even in a house. Anyone wishing to study bats at close quarters must possess a licence issued by English Nature (or the equivalent body in other parts of the UK). One may, however, carefully remove a bat which strays into the living area of a house and injured bats may be cared for until they recover (in practice this is very difficult and the assistance of a veterinary surgeon or some other expert should be sought). If bats occupying a domestic property are unwanted no action to exclude them can be taken without the agreement of English Nature.

Bats are not quite so elusive as casual observation suggests and for those with an interest in seeing them at first hand opportunities do exist. They can be observed in flight without causing disturbance (and therefore without possession of an English Nature licence). This can be done simply by being in the right kind of habitat at a suitable time of day during the summer months. The first hour or two after sunset is the best time to look for bats, when daylight is fading and they are becoming active. Suitable habitats are indicated in the species descriptions in the previous chapter, together with notes which should enable a careful observer to identify many of the commoner species with some degree of certainty. Even some of the most basic facts about the habits of bats are unknown and much remains to be learnt simply by patient observation.

Searching for roost sites is possible but it is time-consuming and care must be taken not to disturb bats, particularly during hibernation. Caves, mineshafts and similar places can be very dangerous and should not be visited by anyone other than an expert. Summer roosts in buildings can sometimes be located by an accumulation of droppings beneath the access point. Bat droppings are about 5 to 15 mm ($^1/_5$ to $^3/_5$ inch) long, depending on the species, roughly cigar-shaped and dark brown or black. When dry they crumble easily to a fine powder, unlike mouse droppings, which become very hard.

For those wishing both to see bats and to

25. *Roost site occupied by about a hundred Pipistrelles during the summer months. The bats roost behind the soffit boards beneath the guttering, gaining access through a small gap between the horizontal board and the brickwork above the window.*

26. *Pipistrelle droppings on the window sill beneath the roost site illustrated in 25 above.*

assist with their conservation, ample opportunity exists because most parts of Britain now have a County Bat Group. These are voluntary bodies, often part of the relevant County Wildlife Trust. The nearest bat group can be contacted via the latter or by writing to the Bat Conservation Trust (address below). Since it is necessary to have a licence even to make observations which may disturb bats, joining a bat group is the best course of action for a genuinely interested person to take. Activities undertaken by these groups vary but usually include visiting roosts in houses to talk to the owners, especially if some problem with the bats arises, catching bats by hand net at roost sites for identification and study and generally promoting bat conservation. Some groups have ongoing studies such as ringing investigations or surveys using 'bat detectors', instruments which convert echolocation sounds to frequencies audible by humans. The calls made by the various species are distinctive, making it possible to identify bats in flight. Some groups have organised schemes to erect bat boxes. These are similar in appearance to bird nest boxes but with the entrance on the underside. They are quite easy and inexpensive to make and details of their construction are contained in a leaflet called *Bat Boxes* available from the Bat Conservation Trust (address below). By working with knowledgeable bat group members, first-hand experience of these fascinating animals can be gained and it is possible to make a significant practical contribution to wildlife conservation.

Further reading

Corbet, G. B., and Harris, S. *The Handbook of British Mammals*. Blackwell, 1991.
Greenway, F.R., and Hutson, A.M. *A Field Guide to British Bats*. Bruce Coleman,1990.
Hill, J.E., and Smith, J.D. *Bats: A Natural History*. British Museum. Natural History, 1984.
Hines, J., and Hines, M. *The Secret World of Bats*. Methuen, 1986.
Ransome, R. *The Natural History of Hibernating Bats*. Christopher Helm, 1990.
Richardson, P. *Bats*. Whittet, 1985.
Robertson, J. *The Complete Bat*. Chatto and Windus, 1990.
Schober, W. *The Lives of Bats*. Croom Helm, 1984.
Schober, W., and Grimmberger, E. (edited by R.E. Stebbings). *A Guide to Bats of Britain and Europe*. Hamlyn, 1989.
Stebbings, R.E. *Which Bat Is It?* The Mammal Society and the Vincent Wildlife Trust, 1986.
Stebbings, R.E. *Bats*. Second edition, Mammal Society, London, 1992.
Stebbings, R.E. *Conservation of European Bats*. Christopher Helm, 1988.
Yalden, D.W. *The Identification of British Bats*. The Mammal Society, 1985.

USEFUL ADDRESSES
The Bat Conservation Trust, 45 Shelton Street, London WC2H 9HJ.
English Nature, Northminster House, Peterborough, Cambridgeshire PE1 1UA.

ACKNOWLEDGEMENTS
Illustrations reproduced by courtesy of Frank Lane Picture Agency are acknowledged to: S. Bisserot, cover, 10, 11, 14, 17, 19, 20; Silvestris GmbH, 18; and by courtesy of Natural Science Photos to: F. Greenway, 3, 4, 9; G. Kinns, 8, 13, 15, 16. All other illustrations are by the author.